P9-CME-578

FRANCE

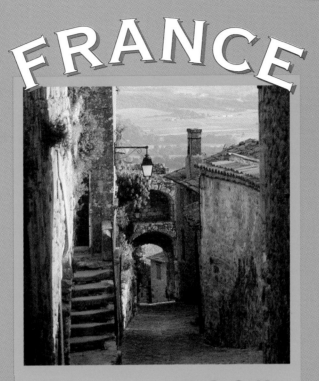

A TRUE BOOK

by

Elaine Landau

Children's Press®

A Division of Grolier Publishing

New York London Hong Kong Sydney
Danbury, Connecticut

Reading Consultant
Linda Cornwell
*Coordinator of School Quality
and Professional Improvement
Indiana State Teachers
Association*

Author's Dedication
For Michael

A French lavender field

**Visit Children's Press® on the
Internet at:**
http://publishing.grolier.com

Library of Congress Cataloging-in-Publication Data

Landau, Elaine.
France / by Elaine Landau.
    p.   cm. — (A True book)
    Includes bibliographical references and index.
    Summary: Describes the geography, history, culture, and people of
France, the largest country in Western Europe.
    ISBN: 0-516-21173-0 (lib. bdg.)   0-516-27023-0 (pbk.)
    1. France Juvenile literature. [1. France.] I. Title. II. Series.
DC17.L36   2000
944—dc21   99-14956
                                                                              CIP

Contents

The city of Paris at night

A Country in Europe

France is a country in Europe with an area of 210,026 square miles (543,965 square kilometers). It's a little smaller than the U.S. state of Texas. France is known for fine food. It is also an outstanding art and fashion center.

The capital of France is Paris, which is known as the City of Lights. It is also considered by many to be one of the world's most beautiful cities. But there's much more to France. The country has snow-capped mountains, fishing villages, sunny beaches, and a lovely countryside dotted with orchards and vineyards. Indeed, there are many sides to France.

A Varied Landscape

France may seem small compared to the United States, but it's the largest country in western Europe. The bodies of water bordering France are the North Sea, the Strait of Dover, the English Channel, the Atlantic Ocean, and the Mediterranean Sea.

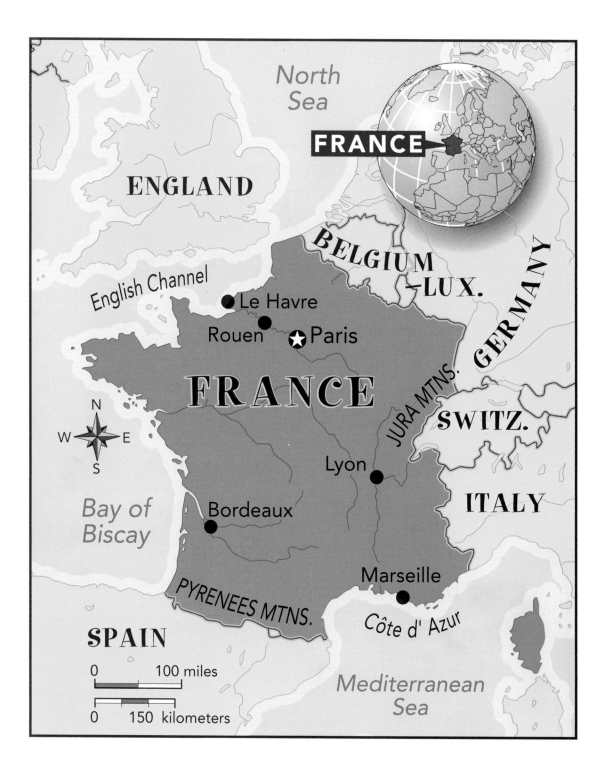

The Côte d'Azur (koht-duh-sur), known to most tourists as the Riviera, lies on France's Mediterranean coast. Towns along the Riviera often have brightly painted houses and beautiful gardens. The area has many lemon, orange, fig, and imported palm trees.

In other regions of France, forests are enormous. More than one hundred and thirty different types of trees grow in the forests of France, because of the various climates.

The climate in France varies in different regions. Along the Mediterranean Sea, people enjoy warm weather throughout the year. Other areas in France are cool in the winter with highs of about 45° Fahrenheit (7° Celsius). Summers tend to be warm with highs of about 80° F (27° C).

Paris is France's largest city. More than 9 million people live in Paris and the surrounding area. France has many other large cities. Marseille, Toulouse, and Lyon are among twelve French cities with populations of more than 350,000 people. Twenty other French cities have more than 200,000 inhabitants. The total population of France is about 58,600,000.

France is separated from Italy by the Alps mountain range. At the border between

A ski resort nestled in the French Alps.

France and Switzerland are the Alps and Jura Mountains. The Pyrenees Mountains divide France and Spain. Other countries bordering France are Germany, Andorra, Monaco, Luxembourg, and Belgium.

Place de la Concorde

The Champs Élysées

Arc de Triomphe

A French cafe

The Champs Élysées (shanz-ay-lee-zay) is an avenue in Paris and one of the city's finest promenades, or walks. The Champs Élysées (French for "Elysian Fields") extends from the Place de la Concorde to the Arc de Triomphe (Arch of Triumph). Famous hotels and the Théâtre de Marigny, line the famous avenue. At the upper end of the avenue near the Arc de Triomphe, busy cafés, shops, hotels, and movie theaters bustle with people. The Champs Élysées is always a favorite stop for both the French and visitors to Paris.

Government

France's government is led by a president who is elected to a seven-year term in office. Like the U.S. president, this person heads the nation's armed forces. France's president also directs foreign policy. The president chooses a prime minister, or premier,

The French Parliament in Paris

who oversees the daily running of the government. Among other duties, the prime minister submits new laws to Parliament. The Parliament is similar to the U.S. Congress.

15

It consists of the National Assembly and the Senate. French citizens elect members of Parliament, just as people in the United States vote for their representatives in Congress. The prime minister also sees that the laws are carried out throughout the country.

France also has a Constitution which guarantees that the country remains free and independent.

History

In ancient times, people known as the Gauls lived in the region now called France. They were conquered by Julius Caesar and the Roman army between 58 and 51 B.C. After the fall of Rome in the A.D. 400s, France was invaded by a number of Germanic tribes from the east.

These included the Franks, after whom France was named. By the A.D. 800s, the French emperor Charlemagne had made France a large and powerful kingdom.

After the 10th century, France was ruled mostly by a

series of monarchs. The monarchy reached its height during the reign of Louis XIV (1638–1715). Known as the Sun King, he built the fabulous Palace of Versailles. But building grand palaces and paying for a series of wars strained France's finances. The rulers who followed Louis XIV continued to tax the people heavily, despite severe food shortages.

In what became known as the French Revolution, the people rose up in protest. On July 14,

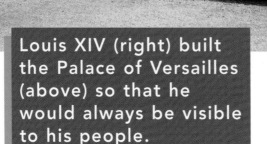

Louis XIV (right) built the Palace of Versailles (above) so that he would always be visible to his people.

1789, crowds stormed an old fortress and royal prison in central Paris called the Bastille. The king, Louis XVI, was overthrown. On September 21, 1792, France was declared a republic.

The new French republic
soon had to defend itself
against attacks from nearby
countries. But French forces
successfully pushed back the
foreigners.

During this time, a young
army officer named Napoleon
Bonaparte had been steadily
gaining power in the military.
He eventually overthrew the
French government and
declared himself emperor.
Napoleon helped strengthen

Napoleon Bonaparte
(1769–1821)

the government of France by changing its administration and legal system. Before his defeat in 1814, he had paved the way for France to become the successful nation it is today.

The People

The families of most of the people who live in France have been there for a long time. The population also includes people who have moved there from Portugal, Algeria, Italy, Morocco, and Turkey.

City people usually live in houses and apartments. Many

People of France

French cities are pleasant and
beautiful. In some places, laws
limit the amount of traffic and the
types of buildings that can be
constructed. But city life can be
expensive. As a result, many
people live on the outskirts of
the cities or in nearby towns.

Only a small portion of French people live in the countryside— on farms and in villages. Some are farmers. They usually live in single-family homes instead of apartments.

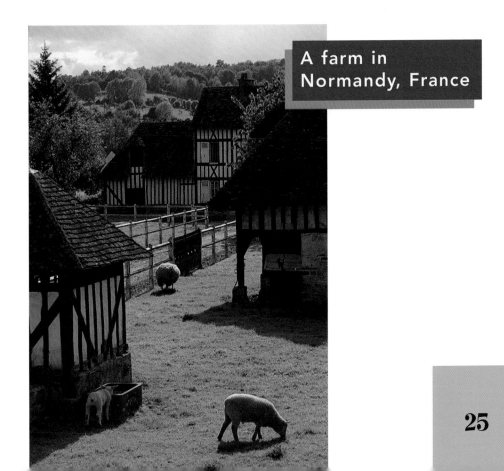

A farm in Normandy, France

French children must attend school from age six to sixteen, but many go to the country's free nursery schools from the time they are three. After high school, some students continue their education at universities. Others attend schools known as grandes écoles (great schools). These schools train students for high-level positions in the military, government, business, engineering, education, and other fields.

Most French people enjoy sports. Many take part in an outdoor sport on a regular basis. The most popular activities include soccer, bicycling, tennis, skiing, basketball, and rugby, which is similar to American football. In 1998, France won the World Cup in soccer.

The Tour de France

The biggest national sporting event in France is a bicycle race called the Tour de France. In this event, held every summer, more than 200 professional cyclists pedal through 2,409 miles (3,877 kilometers) of France and neighboring countries. The race is run in about twenty-five stages and takes three weeks to complete. The finish line is in Paris.

Most French people eat three meals a day. They eat dinner late in the evening, at about 7:00 P.M., and their largest meal of the day is at noon. France is known for its food. French cooking is considered by many to be the best in the world. French chefs have originated such great dishes as a fish stew called bouillabaisse (BU-yah-bez) and escargot (es-car-GO) served in butter sauce. The crisp, skinny loaves of French bread called baguettes (ba-GETS) are famous around the world.

Most of the people in France are Roman Catholics. Smaller numbers of Muslims, Jews, Protestants, and people of other faiths also live there.

Art and Culture

France has a rich cultural heritage. The motion picture camera was invented in France in 1895. Today, many French filmmakers continue to produce excellent films.

France may be best known as an international center for artists. Many creative painting

Monet spent the last ten years of his life painting scenes of his garden, such as *Water Lilies* (above).

styles and trends began in France. Famous French painters include Pierre August Renoir, Claude Monet, and Henri Matisse. Other world-renowned artists who came to

France to paint were Vincent van Gogh, Pablo Picasso, and Joan Miró.

There are more than one thousand museums in France. Millions of visitors tour them each year. The Louvre—one of the world's largest museums—is a "must-see" stop for many tourists.

In addition to holding thousands of works of art, the museum itself is a masterpiece. In 1989, a huge glass pyramid

I. M. Pei's glass pyramid at the Louvre

designed by Chinese-American architect I. M. Pei was opened at the Louvre. It serves as the entrance to the museum and has become a favorite Paris landmark. France also has more than 1,500 monuments. About 5 million people visit the Eiffel

The Eiffel Tower

Located in Paris, the Eiffel Tower is one of the most famous sites in France. Built in 1889 to celebrate the 100th anniversary of the French Revolution, the tower stands 984 feet (300 meters) tall. Visitors can take elevators or stairways to the top. On the way, there are restaurants, a weather station, and great views from the observation platforms.

Tower every year. It is France's most popular attraction.

Theater is also important in France. National theaters, national drama centers, and playhouses put on more than fifty thousand performances a year. In addition, French music has long been praised. Outstanding French composers include Hector Berlioz, Claude Debussy, and Joseph-Maurice Ravel. *Carmen,* by the French composer Georges

Bizet, is among the most-performed operas in the world. France is also a hot spot for jazz, an American musical form. Many American jazz players have moved to France because the French love jazz so much.

The French are famous for their literature, as well. The work of French writers such as Molière, Jean Racine, and Victor Hugo set a high standard. The recent Disney film

More than a century after it was published, *The Hunchback of Notre Dame*, by Victor Hugo (right), was made into a Disney film (above).

The Hunchback of Notre Dame was based on a book by Hugo.

The Economy

France is a prosperous nation. It has the fourth-largest economy in the world, after the United States, Japan, and Germany.

Manufacturing and mining are important to the French economy. It is the world's second-largest exporter of

Dairy products such as cheese (left) and perfume (right) are two of France's leading exports.

aircraft and the fourth-largest exporter of cars. Other products made in France include iron, steel, medicine, computers, radios, televisions, chemicals, cosmetics, textiles, and wine. France is also known for its fine china, glass, and pottery.

The country is a leading producer of farm products, too. Fruits, vegetables, and dairy products (including more than three hundred different types of cheese) are among them. It is also the second-largest exporter of wines. Only Italy produces more.

France has long been considered the fashion capital of the world. Every year, people in the international fashion industry come to see the French designers' latest clothing lines. France is also the number-one perfume exporter in the world. Many French perfumes are famous for their popularity—and their high prices.

The country of France is a land of beauty, history, and

A château in France

culture. A famous American once described the city of Paris as "everyone's second home." Perhaps the same could be said of all of France.

To Find Out More

Here are some additional resources to help you learn more about the country of France:

Books

Benedict, Kitty. **The Fall of the Bastille.** Silver Burdett, 1991.

Gilbert, Adrian. **The French Revolution.** Thomson Learning, 1995.

Hautzig, David. **1,000 Miles in 12 Days: Pro Cyclists on Tour.** Orchard Books, 1995.

Loewen, Nancy. **Food in France.** Rourke Book Co., 1991.

Stein, R. Conrad. **Paris.** Children's Press, 1996.

Venezia, Mike. **Pierre Auguste Renoir.** Children's Press, 1996.

Embassy of France

http://www.info-france-usa.org/index.htm

Maintained by the French Embassy in Washington, D.C., this site was designed specifically for kids. Learn about the history and economy of France, play a French game, or learn the French national anthem.

Koronis-French for Kids

http://www.koronis.com/french/kids/

Impress your friends by learning some common French phrases at this website.

La Tour Eiffel

http://www.tour-eiffel.fr/indexuk.html

At its official website, check out the construction and history of this world-famous landmark. Dare to take a 3-D tour of the Tower, send a virtual postcard to friends, or paint the Eiffel Tower!

Museé du Louvre

http://www.smartweb.fr/louvre/index.html

One of the most famous museums in the world, the Louvre houses the most important art collection in the Western world, with more than three hundred rooms to browse through. Learn about this historical museum, including its new Egyptian rooms.

Versailles

http://www.smartweb.fr/versailles/

Take a complete tour of Château de Versailles without leaving your home!

Important Words

descendant the offspring of a particular person or group

emperor the male ruler of an empire

inhabitants people living in a specific area or region

monarch a person who rules a kingdom or an empire; a king or queen

promenade a leisurely walk in a public place

prosperous successful, wealthy

republic a form of government in which the people have the power to elect representatives who manage the goverment

vineyard an area in which grapes are grown

Index

Meet the Author

Popular author Elaine Landau worked as a newspaper reporter, editor, and a youth services librarian before becoming a full-time writer. She has written more than one hundred nonfiction books for young people, including many books for Franklin Watts and Children's Press. Ms. Landau, who has a bachelor's degree in English and journalism from New York University and a master's degree in library and information science from Pratt Institute, lives in Miami, Florida, with her husband and son.